To V

A vegetarian's journey towards veganism

To Ve or Not to Ve

A vegetarian's journey towards veganism

Gaurav Prinja

TATTVA
PRESS

First published in Great Britain in 2020 by Tattva Press
publishing@tattva.org.uk
www.tattva.org.uk

Copyright © Gaurav Prinja 2020

ISBN: 978-1-9998624-7-3

British Library Cataloguing in Publication Data. A catalogue record for this
book is available from the British Library.

Printed and bound by Clays Ltd.

To my parents, for planting the seeds and nurturing the sapling.

To my wife, for caring for the tree—and pruning it back when required!

To my wonderful daughters, for being the sweetest fruit one could ask for.

Table of Contents

You are what you eat...
or what you don't

Each time would be the same. There would be a sudden sense of nervousness around the table, and perhaps a hint of pity in my inquisitor's eyes as they asked their follow-up question, "Is that a religious thing?" I would feel panic as I realised I was about to be judged — the worst possible feeling as a teenager. My answer would fundamentally change this person's perception of me. And not only the person asking the question, but everyone else sitting at the table with their eyes fixed on me.

The easy answer would have been "Yes", but it would be wrong. At that time[1], I didn't want to be seen as someone who blindly followed a faith — or worse, someone who was "fanatical". An alternative would have been to say, "Oh no, I was

---

1 And even now, I guess!

just brought up that way and never thought to change". Indeed, I gave this very answer the first few times such a situation arose, but I was approaching an age where I was starting to come across as someone who put no thought into making serious lifestyle choices, and I certainly didn't want that. No, I needed a deep, impressive answer to this question. One that didn't insult those who were asking it or make them uncomfortable for making a different choice from me.

"Oh, you're vegetarian?"

The preceding question — or statement, really — would usually come after I had declared my diet, or politely refused to share a dish at a meal with a new group of friends. I may not have known them all that well at that point, but never had I thought that what I chose to put in my mouth would mean the next words out of it would cause me to be judged so severely.

This scenario played out several times in my late teens as I joined new clubs and societies and spent time with them. Yes, I was brought up vegetarian and had never really thought about why I didn't eat meat. Most of our wider family were also vegetarian. Whether we were all vegetarian for religious or cultural reasons is hard to say. On the one hand, we all knew that in Hinduism there is a great deal of respect given to all living beings, so vegetarianism was certainly a logical conclusion. On the other hand, eating meat is not expressly forbidden, and I have plenty of Hindu friends who do so. For a lifestyle choice, I would have to do better than simply saying, "I was brought up vegetarian and never really thought about it". This was especially the case by the time I went to University, where there was an unwritten rule that I should be trying new things.

My personal ethic is rooted in Hinduism. Due to the age and diversity of Hinduism, there are many paths one can follow. In some paths, most broad decision-making is prescriptive—i.e., there are a set of guidelines on what to believe, how to behave, what to eat, etc. For people with great conviction, discipline, and faith, this is a brilliant solution: Simply follow the rules and you will attain *Moksha*, or spiritual release. This isn't quite for me. I try to understand the ethics and philosophy of Hinduism to guide me in making practical decisions in my life. Often the practical prescriptions were laid out for a different place and time. Let's take the concept of Karma: I don't fret about being reincarnated as a dung beetle as part of some universal balance for eating something that may be "forbidden". When it comes to deciding exactly what to eat, I try to consider the pragmatic consequences of my actions.

Reaping what you sow

Almost all children are taught to consider the consequences of their actions. This may start as a simple, "Don't touch the candle, you will get hurt," or a slightly more advanced, "If you have an ice-cream now, then you cannot have dessert after lunch". But even in youth, this extends to a more metaphysical concept—either as Santa's naughty-or-nice list, or a Karmic ledger keeping track of our deeds. Either way, we are taught that we will somehow reap what we sow. For me, this idea is grounded in the Hindu philosophy of Karma, but we don't need to believe in someone or something keeping track of our daily exploits to understand the concept of causality.

We apply this concept flawlessly in simple and direct causal chains in day-to-day life. Most people will check if a vehicle is coming before crossing a road; they are aware of the possible consequences of stepping into traffic without looking. As people grow up, they learn to 'shortcut' or bypass these causal chains — this is a useful step. Those who exercise regularly may tell themselves: *"Exercise releases endorphins, burns calories, builds muscle mass, increases bone density, and improves cardiovascular conditioning. Therefore, in the short term, I will elevate my mood and be able to get a good night's sleep. I will be able to deal with stress better and maintain a healthy weight in the medium term. In the longer term, I will be able to stave off diseases like heart disease and diabetes. In old age, the beneficial chemicals released during years of regular exercise can help to keep my mind sharp. I will have better strength, balance, and bone density so reduce the risk of falls and injury."* I imagine most people shortcut this into, *"Exercise keeps me fit and healthy"*, and so will go for a jog. For someone who is young and generally in good health, this shortened causal chain may not be strong enough. They could argue that they are already fit and healthy so don't need to exercise, but by skipping the details of the longer chain, they have missed out on the longer-term consequences of exercise.

It's all relative

Another two concepts worth acknowledging are relativism and compassion. A lot of decisions that people make in life don't have a single right or wrong answer. When making these decisions, it helps to have access to more facts, but the decision itself is ultimately based on a personal set of beliefs. When there is no strict black and white, there is a scale of grey. Each person will take whatever facts they have and then decide where they will sit on this scale, or where they draw their own personal line of "the right amount for me". If you choose to sit on a different part of the scale from me, then I may feel the need to justify my decision. I may get quite emotional about it as I feel you are saying my decision is "wrong". Because I am basing my decision on a deeply ingrained personal set of beliefs, I may feel that you are attacking those beliefs. Two areas where this tendency is particularly strong are religion and politics. There is no right answer to certain questions in these areas, so one is advised to avoid those topics when making small talk at a party. Let's pick a safer topic of conversation to drive home the concept.

Everyone has a different level of skill and risk aversion when driving. Imagine a relatively empty motorway and ask yourself, "How fast should I drive?" The speed limit is 70 mph, but this is not a target. As a minimum, people will drive around 60 mph. This is a good speed for fuel efficiency; it's also safer, as stopping distances are shorter and the driver has more time to react to the traffic ahead. As you go faster, the journey time decreases, but the fuel efficiency drops, making the journey more costly and polluting. It will also make the journey riskier. The legal speed limit of 70 mph is not often enforced strictly. It is in place as a blanket number to cover all motorways, drivers, and conditions. Some people feel comfortable driving faster than this (at increased cost and pollution and decreased journey time and safety). Setting aside the legal limit, there is really no single right answer for how fast one can *safely* drive. It is a sliding scale, and people will place themselves at different points on this scale. So when a person driving at 70 mph has to change lanes to overtake the car driving at 60 mph, he considers the slower driver an "idiot". But when the same driver is overtaken by someone travelling at 80 mph, he considers the faster driver a "maniac"!

There is an episode of *The Simpsons*[1] that shows this quite nicely in the context of food. The family visits a petting zoo, leading Lisa to decide to stop eating meat. Lisa is generally disgusted with her family and friends for continuing to eat meat, and in her indomitable eight-year-old way, she lets them know this. After taking the moral high ground for most of the episode, upon speaking with Apu she suddenly realises that Apu is disgusted at the idea of eating cheese — it turns out Apu follows a vegan diet! He says, *"I don't eat any food that comes from an animal"*. Lisa suddenly has a realisation. *"You must think I'm a monster"*, she states. This is moral relativism and empathy all rolled into one. She has realised that she currently sits in the middle of this scale, finding her friends and family disgusting based on her personal dietary choice, but also recognizing that Apu as a vegan must feel the same way about her.

Apu's response sums this up nicely: *"I learnt long ago, Lisa, to tolerate others rather than forcing my beliefs on them."*

Whilst writing this book, I have occasionally mentioned to people that I'm writing about veganism. It's interesting how many of them respond by saying that they could never be vegan because there is a particular nutrient that they would be lacking. Or how they tried it but there was one particular product they just couldn't give up. They usually say this before I've even reached the point of telling them that, at the time of writing, I'm not actually vegan myself.

Often, the debate around veganism can get highly charged. This is because, along with politics and religion, many people have deeply held beliefs around diet, and challenging these beliefs can leave people feeling vulnerable. Like Apu, I have no intention of forcing a new diet on anyone. I'm just hoping that by sharing my investigation of veganism I will be able to help you, the reader, to make a more conscious and informed choice about your own diet.

Why am I considering a change?

Over time, my slightly over-indulgent lacto-ovo-vegetarian diet has taken its toll. In my teens and twenties, I was generally active. I preferred to walk or cycle, I had time to play sports, and I took stairs rather than lifts — in fact, I generally avoided the gym. I probably ate too much takeaway pizza, almost kidding myself that it was healthy[2]. Once I started work, there was little time for exercise, and taking the stairs up one floor wouldn't compensate for sitting at a desk for ten hours a day. With a slew of medical conditions in my family history[3], and seeing the first signs of them in myself, I began to recognize that, along with regular exercise, I probably needed to rethink my diet.

---

[2] My logic was that in a pizza the base is essentially bread (which provides carbohydrates), it's covered in vegetables (which provide vitamins and minerals) and has cheese (which provides fats and protein). This is probably true of pizza from a traditional Italian pizzeria, but as a student I was getting cheesy, greasy take-away pizza with the crust stuffed with cheese and with extra cheese on top. If you hadn't guessed, I'm a turophile.

[3] Being of Indian origin, diabetes, high blood pressure, and high cholesterol are kind of par for the course.

10

As someone who doesn't smoke, doesn't drink alcohol, didn't snack (sticking with three meals a day), doesn't add salt at the table (preferring to add a bit of chilli powder if I think the food is a bit bland), and can quite happily ignore chocolate and sweets around the house, I was struggling to figure out what was wrong. In analysing my diet, I realised that I was simply overeating at meals, and in those meals, I was not eating the "right stuff". I was already vegetarian, so I was confused — it's not like I could stop eating red meat and fried chicken! It wasn't until I looked closer that I realised most of the things that were "bad" for me stemmed from overdoing it in the animal products department — mainly the fat and cholesterol in eggs and cheese. The cheese on a takeaway pizza also probably meant the salt content was very high.

In striving to be healthier, I checked in at the gym. During the induction, the instructor suggested significantly reducing carbs in my diet to help lose weight. Fair enough. Talking to the doctors about hypertension and rising blood sugar, I was told to eat more carbs from grains, to eat more fruit and vegetables, and spread out my meals with snacks so I'm not overeating at meals. Err, okay... *healthy* snacks. Talking to the dentist, I was told to avoid snacking on fruit regularly as the sugars are bad from my teeth. Eh? Needless to say, the confusion only increased. As with the causal chain shortcut for exercise, I wanted to just be told in simple language, "Eat like this, it is good for you", without having to run through all the minute details of every ingredient of every meal.

I was looking for a healthy diet — not a "do this for four weeks" diet, but a "rules for eating for life" diet. When trying to look for more healthy diet options, a predominantly plant-based diet kept popping up.

In recent years, a number of friends and family have adopted a vegan diet — or indeed veganism as a whole. So I began wondering if I should revise my stance on my diet and lifestyle. As anyone who has ever had to renew their car insurance knows, the best decision made in the past may no longer be the best decision for you today. It is good practice to revisit past decisions and reassess them.

Imagine, if you will...

Let's go back to the choice of what goes into one's mouth. If we consider causal chains, then the downstream chain mainly relies on biology and science to determine the effects of what we consume on our bodies. I have to admit, this was only a minor concern for me, so my diet hasn't been ideal from the point of view of its longer-term effects on my body. The upstream chain is more moral. Before putting something in your mouth, do you consider what it is and where it came from? In particular, if you had the raw ingredients (and the skills and time), would you be happy to follow through the processes involved in putting the meal on the table? In my late teens, I thought hard about my diet and eventually developed this thought experiment to explain my vegetarianism to those who asked.

You are walking home late one evening, all the restaurants and shops are closed. You've not eaten since lunch, but there is no food at home. You can go shopping in the morning and can get whatever you like to eat at that point. Along the way, you come across a field with a sign saying, "Help yourself for free". In this field are apple trees, would you take some apples and eat them?

In this scenario, most[4] people would say "*yes*". Now we change the scenario, replacing the trees with wheat, onions, tomato vines, herbs, a cow, and some yeast. Assuming I have the relevant skills and tools (and the ability to speed up certain natural processes), I would be happy to harvest the wheat, grind it into flour, grow a yeast culture, and make some dough. I'd be happy to milk the cow and use the milk to make cheese. I'd have no objection to picking the leaves from the herbs (aware that this damages the plant), harvesting the onions (aware that it kills the plant), or taking any of the other fruit/vegetables. I'd happily make a pizza and eat it. Most non-vegans would probably

---

4 I tried this scenario with a former girlfriend who would occasionally eat meat. She said "*no*" to eating the apples. It turns out she had Oral Allergy Syndrome, a strange condition where uncooked apples cause an allergic reaction but apples crumbles do not! As a result she made amazing baked desserts - she is now my wife.

say "Yes" to this as well. If you remove the cheese, then I think most vegans would also be happy with this scenario.

One final iteration to the scenario: the field now contains a pig and a knife. I would not feel comfortable killing the pig and having some bacon. I'd rather stay hungry until the next day. I'd wager no vegetarian or vegan would be happy to kill the animal themselves to eat it. There will be those who are happy to look the pig in the eyes and kill it to satiate their hunger for a few hours. There are also many people who would be happy to pick up some bacon rashers at the supermarket the following morning but would be uncomfortable *killing the pig themselves* in this scenario. These people have not considered the causal chain leading up to their consumption of meat. Remember that everyone draws a line on what they eat in a different place. Perhaps those who would be comfortable with killing and eating the pig may draw a line if the animal in the field was a dog or a horse.

Now let's address some other common hypothetical questions asked of vegetarians or vegans If I was deserted on an island and the only food source was an animal (assuming the animal feeds on something inedible for humans), then personally, yes, I would kill and eat the animal. It would be the only way to survive. If I ever found myself in that situation, I would be using the guidelines set out in the SAS Survival Handbook[2] which says, "No part of a carcass should be wasted". I'd bleed the animal and keep the blood — it's very nutritious. After skinning the animal, I'd make use of the offal, and only then move onto the actual cuts of meat. This is not how most people consume meat in the modern-day because they are not in a survival situation. Luckily, neither am I. I have plenty of other food sources around, so I don't need to kill and eat animals to survive. What if the animal was dead already? If I didn't need it to survive, then personally, I still wouldn't eat it.

Taking this one step further, if you and your friends were deserted somewhere with no other source of food, would you eat each other? Even if one of your friends was already dead? Most people would baulk at this idea, most likely stating (much like my being on a desert island),

"Yeah, but that could never happen". I'm sure if you asked the passengers of Uruguayan Air Force Flight 571 the same question before 1972, they would have found the idea abhorrent. However, after their plane crashed on a glacier in the Andes Mountains, and they were faced with a complete absence of food, they chose to eat their dead friends to survive. As far as I know, none of them have continued eating human flesh after they were rescued and other food sources became available. Thus, if something is an acceptable food source in a survival situation, it does not mean we have to make it part of our normal diet.

Until now, these thought experiments have worked quite well for me as a vegetarian, but when I consider my dairy intake, I'm imagining a happy, healthy cow whom I treat nicely and from whom I only take a bit of excess milk. I have no objection to this, but in reality, this is not how the milk available in most shops is obtained. Perhaps I need to start considering the broader implications of my actions — the indirect consequences of my decisions. No one has objections to buying clothing in general, but they may choose to avoid brands that are known to exploit child labour. Compared to the options nearly twenty years ago, when I last really reconsidered my diet, the availability of vegan products has increased massively. Since I was already a vegetarian, the question for me was whether I was still comfortable with (and morally justified) in my consumption of dairy and eggs.

Feasting, fasting, and philosophy

The Vegan Society[1] defines veganism as follows:

Veganism is a way of living which seeks to exclude, as far as is possible and practicable, all forms of exploitation of, and cruelty to, animals for food, clothing or any other purpose.

This is not just a diet; it is a philosophy for how to live your life. This belief system then becomes part of how someone chooses to eat. I find this interesting. There is a principle in Hinduism of *ahimsa,* meaning non-harm, and there is also a belief that all living creatures have a spark of divinity—essentially a soul. Hindu texts often suggest avoiding meat, as it can only be obtained by killing an animal. As such, a lot of people assume that most Hindus are vegetarian, but in fact, there is no strict diet prescribed in Hinduism, and even those texts that recommend avoiding meat include caveats for when eating meat is permissible. For instance, the Brahmasutra in chapter 3 section 4 verse 28 states, *"And the permission of all food (is valid) in the event of danger to life"*. Due to the breadth of the historical texts and the vast regional differences in India, many dietary practises have evolved over time. Bearing this in mind, many (but certainly not "most") Hindus do follow a vegetarian diet.

There is little data identifying diet by religion, but the population of India is approximately 80% Hindu[2], and about two-thirds of the country do consume some form of meat[3]. As a rough measure, this means that at least 16% and at most only 41% of Hindus are vegetarian—so certainly less than half. To put this into context, however, the number of vegetarians in India is approximately 70% more than the number of vegetarians in all other countries *put together*[4].

It is important to understand some broader Hindu philosophy to see how it may be applied to diet. This is no small task as there are mountains of literature in Hinduism, so let's try to find a simple explanation. Ancient Hindu texts are generally written in Sanskrit and are difficult to interpret. Over time, there have been many different translations into English, so in explaining these I have merged a number of different translations and interpretations to give a feel for what is being said.

Mohandas Karamchand Gandhi famously stated, *"If all the Upanishads and all the other scriptures happened all of a sudden to be reduced to ashes, and if only the first verse in the Isha Upanishad were left in the memory of the Hindus, Hinduism would live forever."* So let's start there.

The verse essentially states three main principles about the world. First is the idea that "God" is infinite and all-pervading—meaning there is a bit of this divine spark in us and also in everything else in the world. I'm using the word "God" for simplicity, but the concept is not necessarily a personification of a supreme being, rather an all-pervading supreme energy. Second, there is an instruction to renounce—or at least minimise—our use of things. Finally, there is a proscription against coveting because, ultimately, we do not "own" anything.

Another question worth asking is, "What is the job of human beings in relation to the planet?"

This is where there was a little bit of divergence from the generally accepted interpretation of the other major faiths. All major faiths agree that God's hand was behind creation in some way, shape, or form. When we try to investigate the relationship between people and the planet, in the Abrahamic faiths the words used are "the lord of the creatures", or having "dominion over creation". One may interpret this to say that as a "king" has dominion, he also should "protect" his subjects. This sentiment is much better popularised by Stan Lee through the Spiderman franchise: "With great power, comes great responsibility". But essentially "Man" was told he was in charge on earth.

The Hindu scriptures use a different word completely. The Aitareya Upanishad describes creation, and after the first two verses where the different worlds are created, the third verse states:

"He thought, 'Here then are the worlds. Let me now create the guardians of the worlds.' From the waters themselves, he drew forth the person and gave him a shape."

The word used in Sanskrit is *Lokpaalaan*, breaking down literally to 'world'-(*lok*) and 'protect'(*paalaan*)—similar to the modern Hindi word *paalan*, meaning 'to nurture', or 'bring up'. First, here we note that human beings are acknowledged as being part and parcel of nature—*we are made from it*. Secondly, the job description of human beings is 'protectors of the world'.

Now, one needn't take these writings literally. In the past, people respected the sun based on their observations. It would be revered as *Surya Devta* in ancient India or *Ra* in ancient Egypt. If someone walked through a desert in the burning sun, they would probably quite quickly fold their hands towards it and ask for mercy! Admittedly, we all know that the sun is nothing but a ball of gas and dust undergoing nuclear fusion—how mundane to know the secret! We have air-conditioned cars and buildings to avoid the burning heat. At the same time, the Sun is still worthy of reverence. It is the source of life for this planet; if there was no sun, there would be no human life on the planet.

Many ancient cultures personified natural forces. For instance, the Greeks would worship Poseidon before a sea voyage praying for favourable sailing conditions. Although now we have far better systems of monitoring the weather and naval conditions, I think you'd be hard-pressed to find a sea captain who did not respect the power of the oceans.

As such, if we try to take the overarching message from these texts, we are left with a few simple pragmatic principles.

First of all, we are part of an interconnected natural world. Being interconnected means that every action one chooses to take will have some repercussions. As I stated earlier, we need not think about a metaphysical ledger that will come back and bite us for our actions. Just think scientifically, practically, and consciously about the causal chains leading to and from our decisions in that moment.

Second, in modern times, we tend to see ourselves as the apex of evolution and consider ourselves "better than the animals." We have developed a mentality that nature and science must be mastered and bent to our will, but in the Hindu tradition, it is understood that we are part of nature (in fact are responsible for its protection). These traditions attest that whilst we should learn about the workings of the universe, we shouldn't fail to preserve it and show it the correct respect.

Third, Hindu scripture emphasises that we should only use what we need from nature. Basically, we should avoid overindulging. Again, this makes sense; if we suddenly demand too much electricity, then the demand will most likely be met by burning more fossil fuels (at least in our current moment). We humans are a resourceful bunch and we are coming up with new methods to generate electricity that don't involve burning fossil fuels and releasing more carbon into the atmosphere. However, until those alternatives become more prevalent, perhaps we should be more careful with our use of electricity?

Rules and rituals

I recall making a pilgrimage to the Vaishno Devi Temple in India. The temple is located in a cave on a mountainside. Traditionally, a visitor starts in the town of Katra and climbs 700m over a twelve-kilometre path. It is said that anyone who makes the journey will have their prayers answered — with the effort of the climb being almost like a test of faith or a penance to earn a boon from the Mother Goddess. A couple of hours set aside for mindful reflection whilst hiking up the path is probably also helpful. I enjoy hiking, so for me it was a fun expedition and I liked the exercise; I am happy for the Mother Goddess to grant me nothing more than the ability to try to make the best decisions in my life and the courage to face their consequences. Along the way we saw some people had hired *paalkis*. This is a service offered where four men carry a passenger on a chair so that they needn't walk up the path themselves. The intention of these is to help the infirm, but I did see one apparently able-bodied, if somewhat rotund, gentleman climbing into one after walking back from a coffee stall.

Now, perhaps he had an invisible medical condition meaning his exercise tolerance was very low. I am willing to give him the benefit of the doubt, but it certainly made me wonder. If a perfectly able-bodied person decided to hire a *paalki* to make their way to the temple, then would their wishes be granted? Or would the four carriers (even if they didn't enter the temple) get all the good juju for doing the climb? This was an amusing diversion to talk about on our way up the mountain. On a pragmatic level, this is a bit silly. This person would be dogmatically sticking to a cultural tradition (e.g., that visiting the temple proves your faith), but they would be doing it in a way that is the most convenient for themselves by avoiding the traditional "payment" (walking up themselves) by getting someone else to do it for them. Ultimately, the whole point of the exercise is missed. It has just become a mindless ritual that that person has undertaken without thinking about the practical impact on the four carriers[5]. This would be someone who lets their beliefs about the unknown metaphysical consequences of their actions supersede the consequences of their actions on other people in the world right now.

------

[5] There is also a helicopter service to take you up the mountain. Admittedly it is very expensive, but if someone felt they absolutely had to visit the temple, they could do it without burdening someone else with the labour of the climb.

What we consider as "Hinduism" today is actually a combination of many "religions", i.e. lots of different systems of faith and style of worship. They are all, however, based on a common set of principles or philosophies. These principles were generally what informed people's world views, and over time, different practices emerged based on the levels of understanding and technology. This is why for almost every practice in "modern" Hinduism, someone will be able to "quote a scripture" to say it is wrong. Likewise, for any scriptural reference, there will be another translation claiming the previous one was misinterpreted!

According to some translations, certain texts speak of animal sacrifice, but these practices have largely been abandoned as the practises and rituals evolved over time. Take the Manava Dharmashastra, popularly known as the Manusmriti and often translated as the "Laws of Man". This is considered by some as a set of rules that govern how to live, but it was compiled based upon the lifestyle nearly two thousand years ago. The start of Chapter 5 deals with diet. Interestingly enough, it doesn't explicitly forbid the eating of meat, and it contains a lengthy list of different types of food, but it is all based on that time and region. For instance, there is no mention of kangaroo meat, as no kangaroos existed in India two thousand years ago.

Meat eating is said to be allowed under certain circumstances. Chapter 5, verse 31, states that the consumption of meat is permitted as part of a sacrifice, but to persist with using meat on other occasions is not. It continues in verses 45-48, advising against injuring harmless animals for pleasure, eventually noting that meat can only be obtained by injuring sentient beings, so meat should be avoided. Before moving onto a new topic, the final verse on food (Chapter 5, verse 56) states categorically that there is no sin in eating meat, but that *abstention brings great rewards*.

For someone who studies these texts, it can be quite confusing about exactly which rituals or traditions to follow. The Chandogya Upanishad (Chapter 1, section 10) relates the story of Ushasti, a knowledgeable but poor priest. In this story, Ushasti's crops have failed and he and his wife are hungry. He goes to wealthy village (described in the story as very wealthy because the people there owned elephants). Starving, Ushasti goes to a man who is eating some beans and asks for some food. (In the story, this man is referred to as *ibhyam,* or an elephant driver. I was going to translate this as "Elephant Man", but for brevity, let's call this other character "Jo".) Jo says that the leftovers on his plate are all that remain of the beans. Ushasti asks to have them anyway, so Jo gives them to him and also offers the rest of his water. This time, Ushasti refuses, saying drinking the water would be taking the leftovers of another person, which is prohibited by tradition. Confused, Jo asks, "*Are these beans not also leftovers?*" Ushasti agrees but points out, "*I could not live if I did not eat these. The drinking of water is at my will*". Most commentaries point out that Ushasti knew it is considered acceptable to break the "rules" if it is a matter of survival and there is no other option. He was permitted to eat the second-hand beans as there was no other food source. However, water would be available from any nearby stream, so taking the water from Jo would not be permitted. Later in the story, Ushasti tells some other priests that if they perform rituals without understanding them properly, their heads will fall off. I found this an amusing way to warn against mindlessly performing rituals.

This story highlights an important practical point. You should *understand* the rules well enough to follow the principles behind them, not necessarily the letter of them. Basically, you need to know when it is alright to break the rules.

This is all very complicated. Most people won't read lots of scriptures or debate philosophy — they want to get on with their lives. As such, the essence of the principles is woven into the culture, rituals, and lifestyle. Ultimately, the environment in which many of these texts were composed was ancient and agricultural. Animals were needed to help with daily work, but there was also respect for them.

Mealtime prayers

There are several different mealtime prayers that Hindus use. Some of the more popular ones are from the Bhagavad Gita, the Yajur Veda, and the Taittiriya Upanishad. Few Hindus will read these scriptures in detail, and most rely on simple prayers and rituals to remind them of certain principles. Let's investigate these and see if we can glean an idea of the view of food and eating.

In Bhagavad Gita 4:24, the verse alludes to the philosophy of omnipresence: *God is the food we eat, the hunger we feel, and the process by which we consume and digest the food.* Usually, this verse is followed by another from much later in the Gita: *I reside in all living beings as the digestive fire. I digest the four types of foodstuffs eaten by them as an offering to me* (15:14). So the very act of eating is seen as making an offering to God. This relates back to the earlier verse; if God is the hunger, and is being sated by the food, then the very act of eating is an offering God[6].

In the Yajur Veda 11:83, there is a slightly more pragmatic mealtime prayer: it addresses the *giver of food*, asking that *the food that we consume be nutritious and healthy.* Then it says, *The giver of food should continue onward* (in some translations *across the oceans*), *providing for all living beings.*

---

6 By this argument, one may decide that only the best offerings (such as sweet treats) should be eaten as an offering to God. It should be noted, however, that God does not consume the calories on your behalf!

To put this into a bit more context, when a lot of translations say "all living beings", they are translating the phrase *dvipade chatushpade*. The root word *pad* means "foot", and the other parts of the words are numbers (*dve* means two, and *chatvaari* means four). So the prayer is asking that nutritious food be available for all two-footed and four-footed creatures, showing benevolence to animals and reminding us that part of our remit is to wish goodwill upon them. We have returned to the idea that all life is to be respected (even though the insects and arachnids seem to have been omitted from the list). Another common prayer comes from the Taittiriya Upanishad at the start of the second chapter[7]. The most appropriate translation for mealtimes would be one asking that we: *Protect one another. Eat and work together. Study together to be bright and successful.* Ending by asking that we should *not hate each other*.

Here we have a general message of oneness and cooperation, but I imagine it is the line in here

---

7 I've seen many sources claim that it is Chapter 2 , Section 2 Verse 2 of the text, but in the version I have checked[5] this particular verse appears as an invocation at the start of chapter 2. Therefore it is not numbered with a section or verse.

about eating together that makes it a common mealtime prayer. From reading the texts, my personal feeling is that this one is a bit easier in terms of pronunciation.

In a few brief pages, we've hopefully gotten a feel for how food is thought about in Hindu philosophy. We have skipped over a lot of very specific practises, such as avoiding certain foods on certain days and fasting for special festivals, as they are ritualistic in nature and don't necessarily inform us about the "lens" through which we are looking at food. Equipped with this knowledge, we now want to examine the factors behind choosing a vegan diet and see if we can focus well with our new pair of glasses.

Choices, choices

When choosing what to eat, there are some factors that go beyond "I'm hungry" and "This tastes good". Some will be obvious, but there are some here that I hadn't really considered until I started consciously doing some research. I hope you will find something here that you hadn't considered before and use it to make more informed choices.

Health

I am not a qualified nutritionist, so as a layperson trying to research the effects of a vegan diet, the main message seems to be, "Animal products are bad for you, so eat plants". This is an oversimplification, but diet is complex, so this is the simplest "short-cut" message to take away. We all know that too much fat, sugar, salt, protein (even oxygen[8]) is bad for you. But each of these is essential for you in moderation. I know very fit and healthy people on omnivorous diets and plenty of unhealthy vegetarians. I don't know enough vegans personally to be able to infer their state of health in general (most of them switched from an unhealthy diet to a vegan diet and have seen benefits, but this may be as simple as stopping their unhealthy diet). There are, however, a number of professional athletes who opt for a vegan diet[1],[2] so it is possible to be super fit and healthy without consuming animal products.

Another consideration is frequency. Veganism completely cuts out animal products. Many people who make the switch to a fully plant-based diet claim to see amazing benefits in just a few weeks. If you're vegan and occasionally consume a bit of dairy, eggs or even meat, it probably isn't bad for you in the long run. If our philosophy is not one of strict abstinence but, like the Ishopanishad states, one of minimising our use of

---

8 That's right, no oxygen for a couple of minutes will kill you, but too much will do the same![3]

animal products, then imagine if that person ate one non-plant-based meal per month. The benefits of a purely plant-based diet would persist most of the time. One egg, one glass of milk, or indeed some meat may well have some negative effects on the body, but those negative effects may quickly be reversed after a few days of purely plant-based food. Let's consider something "bad" as an example.

Binging on food (a packet of sweets/vegan-pizza/whatever) means you have ingested far more calories than your body needs over the next few hours, but by your next mealtime, you may well feel hungry and eat a normal meal. The body will use some of the energy from the binge immediately. Some of it is stored as glycogen for short-term use. The rest of the energy is stored as fat in your body[9]. Binge too often, and you will keep storing this excess energy and put on weight. If you reduce the volume and frequency of the food you eat, then your intake of energy over a week is reduced and will get used up. The

---

9 This is based on my memory of GCSE Biology. It was over twenty years ago, but I hope the workings of the human body haven't changed since then!

problem comes from over-indulging and doing so too often. It's easy to over-indulge by telling yourself it's just "once in a while", but over time, we become less aware of actions as they slowly turn into habits, then we wonder why we're burdened with the consequences.

Of course, knowing how much is too much from a health point of view is subjective. For someone who already restricts their consumption of animal products to once every few days, a purely plant-based diet for six days a week would seem like a sensible reduction, and they may notice some health benefits. However, for someone who eats animal products three times a day, reducing to a few times a week may mean they also see some benefits. But this second person would only get as far as the starting point of the first person.

Biology

Biological or anatomical arguments for a purely plant-based diet usually revolve around two main factors. One addresses why we shouldn't eat meat, these are usually attempts to show that humans are non-carnivorous due to the types of teeth and digestive systems we have. There is another argument for avoiding dairy. The statistic that nearly two-thirds of the world is lactose intolerant is often given as evidence that humans aren't supposed to drink milk after weaning. This argument also points out that humans appear to be the only animal that drinks the milk of another species.

In my view, these are oversimplifications. One of the reasons you are here and reading this is that over millennia our species has evolved to eat many different kinds of food. There are plenty of plants that are indigestible or indeed toxic for humans — imagine evolving in an area high in these plants or where vegetation, in general, was scarce. Our ancestors would naturally have had to resort to eating meat to survive. While it is probably true that plants are ingested more safely and digested more efficiently, in a survival situation, meat, milk and eggs are relatively calorie-dense forms of food. To be clear, most people who consume these products are not currently living in a survival situation. When looking through history, we see that humans across the world have eaten meat for thousands of years, and it hasn't caused us to die out. Hindu philosophy advises reducing or avoiding meat consumption as more thought is given to the source of the food. Ultimately, the human body could ingest and digest a whole host of things that most people don't eat — from grass to horses or even other people! Just because we have evolved the ability to eat something doesn't mean we should eat it all the time when other more suitable foods are available.

What about being an outlier by consuming the milk of another species? We are outliers in many other senses, as well. We have highly developed cognitive abilities. We have built cities, machines that allow us to travel faster than any other animal, to fly, even go to the moon. None of this justifies drinking the milk of another species. It is just to point out that if we stuck with that was completely "natural", then we would not have done any of these other things either. The point is this: given that we have the cognitive ability to do so much more than our ancestors, we should use that ability to critically review what we are doing. As potentially the most intelligent form of life on the planet, we can make decisions that supersede basic instincts. We should also be able to consider the broader consequences of our actions and consciously make decisions that are of broader global benefit.

Conditioning

Why do most people not eat grass or horses? This is simply conditioning, or what I like to think of as the "yuck factor". Some vegetarians say the thought of eating meat makes them feel physically sick. In the UK, most omnivores would happily eat "common" meats such as beef and chicken, but tell them that the tasty dish they just ate contained cat or rats, and they may feel nauseated. I was brought up as lacto-ovo-vegetarian, so am comfortable eating eggs, dairy products, and most plants[10]. This is usually based on culture and upbringing. It also requires a bit of thinking to really understand where what you eat is coming from. Perhaps after thinking about the true source of something, you may decide to add or remove it from your diet.

---

[10] I have to admit I don't particularly have an objection to meat being on the table. I recall in my youth my grandfather taking us to McDonalds, and due to the lack of vegetarian options, we would get a hamburger "without the meat". Conversely, I really can't stand aubergine!

Consider mushrooms as an example. In traditional Hindu thought, they grow in "dirty places" and are therefore not something to eat. In ancient times it would be sound advice to avoid eating something that is growing somewhere dirty. Now we know that whilst mushrooms are a fungus, many varieties are safe to eat and are grown on farms.

A great example of this "yuck factor" is an episode of *Friends*[11][4] where Phoebe and Joey taste some breast milk from a bottle. Ross, Chandler, and Rachel (ostensibly the more "educated" members of the group) are disgusted by the action. Rachel goes so far as to point out, *"That is juice squeezed from a person"*. She's not wrong, just as a friend of mine at university wasn't entirely wrong when describing an egg as a *"chicken period"*. These descriptions attest to where certain foods have come from. Then it depends on whether your personal "yuck factor" will allow you to group those foods as edible or not. Later in

---

11 Before looking up the details of the episode, I was trying to remember which one it was and naturally thought "It's the one with the breast milk". Lo and behold, thanks to the naming convention adopted by the show, the episode is indeed called "The One With the Breast Milk".

the episode, Ross refuses to try the breast milk and says, "*I just don't think breast milk is for adults*".

A good self-improvement technique is to stop and review your habits. Diet is no exception. I reviewed my stance before university and found I was comfortable with the status quo. Others will have reviewed and expanded their diet; perhaps they tried new meat, or a fried egg, or a banana peel (yes, it's actually edible!) for the first time and decided it is *not disgusting*.

Environment

As we discussed earlier, in Hindu philosophy, we are charged with the protection of the world. There is staggering data that shows there is a huge negative environmental impact to keep up with current meat and dairy consumption. Environmentalism can be a trigger for people to change their habits—the reduction in the use of plastics and the increase in low-energy light bulbs and electric vehicles attest to this. However, many people are simply not aware of the environmental impact of their diet and are comfortable to avoid digging. For those willing to grab a shovel and do some research, I would recommend *Comfortably Unaware*[5] by Richard Oppenlander. For our purposes, we'll consider two broad examples.

The animals we use (either for eating or milking) need to be fed, and they consume a lot more food than they ultimately produce. So we need far more space, food, and water to produce animal products than we do to produce plants. In terms of space to feed themselves for one year a person on a vegan diet would use about one-sixth of an acre of land—that's just about one penalty box on a football[12] pitch. Include dairy and eggs in there and the requirement *triples*—that's just under a third of a football pitch. The average meat-eater, however, uses about three acres of land to grow food for themselves and the animals that they eat. That's more than one-and-a-half Premier League football pitches—nearly *twenty times* as much as a vegan[6].

---

12 Soccer to any American readers.

Figure 1: Land required to feed someone for a year in Premier League football pitches

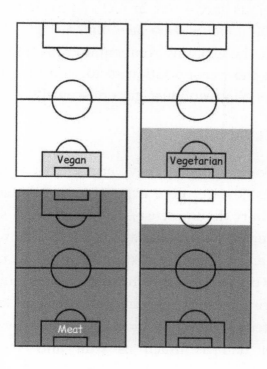

The second startling statistic is for anyone who considers themselves an environmentalist and is trying to fight climate change by driving an electric vehicle and using more public transport. According to the Food and Agriculture

Organization of the United Nations, the livestock sector contributes about 18% of greenhouse gas emissions measured in CO_2 equivalent, stating, *"This is a higher share than transport"*[7]. To cross-check, the U.S. Environmental Protection Agency states the transportation sector contributes about 14% of all greenhouse gas emissions[8].

Economics

Some people may argue that fruit and vegetables are more expensive to eat than meat and dairy. In one sense, they are right. A study[9] conducted a few years ago in the UK showed that fruit and vegetables cost nearly twice as much as dairy per calorie. Unfortunately, in this study meat and fish were thrown in with eggs and lentils as "protein sources", which again collectively cost about half as much as fruit and vegetables. Obviously, the lowest cost-per-calorie were the carbs (bread, potatoes, rice, etc.). Similarly, when trying to assess the cost-per-gram of protein in foods, you will generally find that animal-based products make their way into many "cheapest protein sources" lists[10],[11].

This is the cost to the consumer when buying the products in the supermarket. However, we've just seen in the previous section that animal agriculture uses far more land than plants, and this inefficiency also extends to calories and protein as well. If you harvest plants with 100 grams of protein (or 100 calories of energy) and then sell them, the consumer will buy all the nutrition. If instead you feed those plants to an animal and then sell animal products to a consumer, the consumer only buys a small fraction of the nutrition as shown in this table.

Figure 2: Efficiency of protein and energy conversion[12],[13]

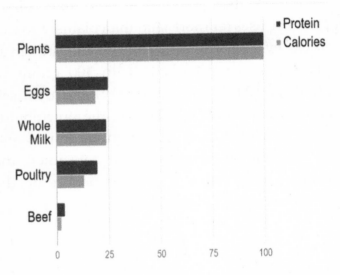

This raises the question: if plant-based foods are so expensive per calorie, and we have to feed animals about five times as many calories of plants to get milk or eggs why are these products not about five times as expensive per calorie? Meats could never be on any top ten lists in terms of cost-per-gram of protein because the plants used to feed the animals in the first place would necessarily make the meat *tens of times* more expensive.

There are two factors to consider here. One is that sometimes animals are fed parts of the plant that humans can't eat. Another factor is that farming is heavily subsidised[14]. Subsidies in the UK have traditionally come from the EU, but post-Brexit, these will come from the UK government, which means the British taxpayer. In fact, the average farmer in England makes more money from subsidies than from selling their produce[15]. Of course, these subsidies are important, and in many cases, they are helping to keep the cost of food artificially low so that the poorest are able to eat. But if the purpose is to make sure no one is going hungry, then surely we would want to be able to feed as many mouths as possible by using the planet's resources to a minimum extent (as per the Isha Upanishad). In other words, we should try to be *efficient*, in which case subsiding animal agriculture seems to be a waste of taxpayer's money if plant agriculture could quite cheaply feed many more mouths.

Quality of life and job creation

What has happened in the UK with meat over the last fifty years or so is similar to what has happened in India with milk over a similar period. In each country the products in question were initially seen as a luxury item only available to the well-off. The middle classes in each country have grown and naturally sought to improve their standard of living, and as such, they have increased the demand for these luxury items. This should have increased the price as well, but governments intervened and artificially boosted supply by either subsidising the product directly or investing in the infrastructure to lower production costs. Whilst the UK government generally took the former approach by subsidising meat farming, India took the latter option.

In India, milk production has exploded[16], making it the largest producer of milk in the world. Behind this glut was Operation Flood[17], a government initiative to increase milk production. Most milk still comes from rural communities, often with a family owning a couple of cows and selling the milk directly to industrial processing centres, giving the rural farmers some additional income. Whilst these families are working in the traditional way of looking after a couple of cows at home, there has been a slight move towards more efficient methods of animal husbandry. More cows are artificially inseminated and given feed rather than being taken to pasture. Older cows cannot legally be slaughtered, but not all farms look after them. We can see why an initiative like Operation Flood would be seen as beneficial when it was started. It would mean more people in the country would have access to milk, and more rural families would have an additional source of income to help if crops fail.

This increase in quality of life is based on people's mind-set. Milk or meat are *perceived* as indicating a higher quality of life because in the past they were hard to come by and were only available to the wealthy. Now we have artificially made these products more readily available, and people have the mind-set that consuming them in ever-increasing quantities means they are better off. And yet, many celebrities[18], who compared to the average person have immeasurable wealth, reject meat and dairy products.

These changes in people's dietary habits didn't happen overnight. Perhaps as more people become aware of the consequences of their diets, the demand for animal products may reduce. Farmers needn't be worried about their livelihoods though. It would not be the first time an industry underwent a drastic change. I loved watching the film *Hidden Figures*[19] (I'm a bit of a nerd[13]), which tells the story of how the installation of (electronic) computers at NASA meant that there was no longer a need for (human) computers[14]. A plucky group of ladies kept their mathematical abilities but also learned FORTRAN (the programming language for the electronic computers) so that they could remain employed. Perhaps government subsidies and programmes can work to include more details about plant-based agriculture when training new farmers to ensure that, over time, they are prepared for the change.

This is precisely what India did over fifty years, making sure rural families were trained to look after cows to allow for an increase in milk

---

13 At a key moment, when a main character suggests using Euler's Method, I knew what that meant.

14 Yep, originally a "computer" was a person who sat and did computations.

consumption. Perhaps now farming communities in India, and across the world, can retrain so that over the next fifty years, the production of animal-based products can be replaced with sufficient plant-based alternatives.

Worth crying over spilt milk?

Milk and yoghurt play an important role in a lot of Indian traditions and Hindu rituals. They are seen as a sign of prosperity, and no doubt this is a throwback to pre-industrial times. If you were wealthier, you would have more cows and therefore access to more milk. Whilst the principle of not harming sentient beings is seen as good practice in India, there has been a long tradition of dairy farming. This seems in contradiction to vegan practice.

The cow holds a special place in Hindu culture. She is venerated as a mother. From a pragmatic point of view, cows provide milk — and therefore butter, yoghurt, cheese and ghee. Their dung can be used as fuel, insulation for mud huts, and fertiliser. Even cow urine was considered useful, working well as fertiliser but less well for its supposed medicinal properties. In death, the cow's skin could be used for leather, and her meat could also be eaten—although after building an effective working (even loving) relationship with the cow, perhaps people would naturally be averse to eating her. Conversely, a cow is usually quite docile and requires very little from humans if allowed to graze and drink. So, it is understandable why a culture of love and respect for the cow arose—she gives so much whilst asking for so little in return.

Although it seems that meat may have been used in rituals and even eaten in ancient India, as the culture evolved, people started re-evaluating their old practices based on their new principles. With the wider spread of Jainism and Buddhism in the last few centuries BCE, more and more people started to consider the cow to be non-edible.

In the Vishnu Purana (Book 1, Chapter 13), there is the story of King Prithu. There is a famine, and Prithu is charged with chasing the "earth" to punish her for not allowing plants to grow. The earth takes the form of a cow to run away but is eventually cornered. The earth then chastises him for trying to kill a female, but his argument is that killing one malignant being to alleviate the suffering of many is permitted. She opines that killing her will mean the death of all his subjects as well, so instead she offers for him to milk her. She tells him that the milk would allow vegetation to be restored.

This is a pretty story, but again, it points out that we're interconnected. Killing the earth dooms us all, so we should only take what we need. Although dating the Puranas is difficult, the Vishnu Purana may well have been compiled in writing after the rise of Jainism and Buddhism, which may have contributed to the idea that cows are not to be killed but to be milked.

Thinking back to the principles behind the culture, we recall that all living beings are considered to have a soul, or *aatmaa*. This was also true of the cow and her offspring. So when a cow would give birth to a calf, it was raised with the mother and allowed to drink milk before the mother was milked for humans. This method of milking is still practised in some rural parts of India where the culture has generally resisted the commoditisation of the cow.

In many parts of the western world, we have almost fully commoditised the cow. It is a machine into which we put feed, water, and occasionally bull semen. It then produces milk which we use machines to extract and female calves which are grown to produce more milk. The waste products are dung, urine, noxious gases, and occasionally, male calves. After a few years, the "machinery" starts to break down and become inefficient, so it is disposed of.

This explains why vegans reject dairy products, whilst in Hindu philosophy dairy is generally regarded as fine to use. Let us dig a bit deeper into veganism. It is not just a diet—it is a belief system that affects a person's daily decisions.

Veganism - Beyond diet

Veganism is essentially a way of life that extends beyond what one eats. Four examples of non-dietary products vegans would avoid are leather, wool, silk, and beeswax. These four are interesting examples which exist at four corners of a "graph". One axis of this graph would be the amount of suffering or exploitation of the animal. The other would be the level of sentience of the animal — i.e., its capacity to experience the world, have feelings, and suffer. Some may consider this to be a binary assumption, stating that obviously a rock is not sentient while all animals are. But sentience is also a scale. I'm going to go with broad strokes here and say that generally larger animals are "more" sentient — they form bonds, they play, they feel pain and fear. As animals (or specifically their brains) get smaller, they probably don't experience emotions as deeply. So, let's run through the four products and see where they sit on the graph.

Clearly, the only way to get leather is by killing and skinning an animal, so aside from health and biology of the consumer, most arguments for veganism would apply here. Someone may be disgusted at the idea of wearing a jacket made of the skin of a dead animal. There is the economic and environmental burden of raising an animal to obtain leather when another material could be used to create a similar piece of clothing. Strangely, wearing fur seems to be acknowledged as cruel even by many non-vegans, while leather shoes, belts, bags, and wallets seem ubiquitous. This may be because leather is a by-product of the beef industry where the animals are already being killed for meat, whereas foxes or beavers would be killed solely for their fur. Thinking back to the causal chain, would you be comfortable with killing a large, sentient, emotional animal to use its skin? Especially nowadays when there is a multitude of faux-leather or other synthetic products available?

Wool comes from shearing off sheep's coats. Sheep are commoditised to meet demand, and whilst shearing can be performed kindly, the process is manual. There are stories of violent mistreatment of sheep, but let's set those aside and say they are probably a minority of special cases. That being said, with any manual process, accidents can happen. One can imagine the shearer will try to get through the process quickly (often being paid per sheep rather than per hour), potentially harming the animal as it wriggles. If you don't think this is plausible, then consider the fact that people occasionally get their ears nicked by barbers using clippers. That's someone who has asked for the process to take place, where both the shearer and 'shearee' know the consequences of a mistake. If you are able to keep yourself aware that a sheep is a living being, and you are charged with its protection, would you be willing to coax it lovingly, treat it gently, and shear it carefully, then use the wool you obtained from it?

Silk production starts to bring the level of sentience into the picture. The *most efficient* method to extract silk generally involves killing the silkworm. The worm is boiled or gassed after forming the cocoon but before it can break out of it. This means longer strands of silk can be unwound from the cocoon. Silk can be extracted by recovering the cocoons after the moth has emerged, but these strands are shorter and are therefore less valuable. A silkworm is probably quite low down on the sentience scale — some may argue that it is not worthy of protection from harm. Looking back at the scriptures, one may argue that when referring to living beings, a common description is "two-footed and four-footed", so insects are not considered to be animals with a soul. Personally, I see these sorts of things as a technicality. I imagine most bipedal and quadrupedal animals (including humans) are more sentient than insects. But rather than getting bogged down with the exact wording, we should consider the spirit of the scriptures and look out for special cases. For instance, octopuses have eight limbs but are considered to be quite intelligent.

Finally, beeswax is produced by bees and can be extracted by taking care not to harm them, but again, this is a manual process. If the beekeeper is careless or rushing, they may kill or maim some of the animals. Related to beeswax is honey, which is also used in Hindu rituals. When extracting honey, some must be left for the colony. Extract too much and the bees have nothing to eat in the winter. Bees probably are sentient (in fact, they are quite clever for their size), but quite low down on the scale, so we have to ask how much we care about these insects[15]? If you were keeping bees, providing them with shelter, and taking all possible care not to harm them when extracting beeswax and honey, then would you object to using the produce?

---

15 Almost as if the universe is trying to test where exactly I draw the line, three wasps have been flying around the room whilst I have been writing. Not wanting to harm them, but afraid they may sting me, I've spent a fair amount of time over the last half-hour trying to guide them toward the open window with a sheet of paper, but they are stubborn. Eventually, I put my convenience first and used a hand-held vacuum cleaner to grab them, knowing this wouldn't be the safest thing for them. When I took the vacuum cleaner outside, two flew away, one went in the bin.

Figure 3: Harm vs Sentience plot

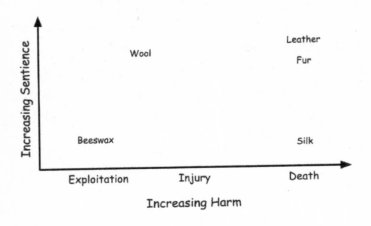

Each individual would be able to draw a line across this graph. I think most practical and compassionate individuals would probably seek to avoid killing highly sentient animals for no reason. Many may accept that sometimes injury or exploitation of animals of reduced sentience is permissible in certain circumstances. Another aspect to consider is the *intention* or the reasoning behind an action. Most people would avoid intentionally hitting a dog with their car. If they accidentally ran over a dog, they would almost certainly feel guilty, and yet they see dead insects on the windscreen as an inconvenience.

To make this a fuller graph, we could include foods and other activities on it. It would also include humans. I imagine most people would put humans at the top of the sentience scale, and moving left-to-right would place actions like slavery, torture, and murder. All meats would be to the right of the graph, above "Death". Animal-derived products like dairy and eggs would go somewhere above injury or exploitation. Sometimes the same product obtained in a different way could go in a different place. Ahimsa silk[1] is made by attempting to avoid harming (or killing) the silkworm, so it would be to the far left of the graph. Milk could be obtained from a naturally lactating cow by milking — but this is not how modern intensive milk production works. Ahimsa milk[2], on the other hand, attempts to take milk without causing undue harm to the animals. There is no artificial insemination and no animals sent to slaughter; calves are left to suckle until naturally weaned, but bulls are castrated so that they are less aggressive. There is still exploitation and a degree of injury (to the bulls), but this ahimsa milk approach is far less harmful than intensive milk production techniques.

Each axis is a sliding scale, and everyone will find themselves in a different place. It's best if people make themselves *consciously aware* of where they are placing themselves on the scale. In her book *Why We Love Dogs, Eat Pigs And Wear Cows*[3], Melanie Joy describes a comparison she often makes with her classes between dogs and pigs. Students generally think of dogs as friendly, intelligent pets with feelings and personalities, whilst pigs are thought of as dirty, stupid animals bred to provide bacon. She then asks the class some questions. When they think about it, the class realises that pigs are actually intelligent, have emotions, and can feel pain. Ultimately, the class tends to surmise that they eat pigs but not dogs because that's "just the way things are" — i.e., they have accepted the status quo without thinking about what they are doing.

In a similar way, about twenty years ago I made myself consciously aware of what I ate and reaffirmed my lacto-ovo-vegetarian diet. Since then, I have just accepted that that is what I eat. Now I am considering a shift to a plant-based diet as I consciously make myself more aware of what I eat.

Veggie to vegan: A leap of faith?

Already being vegetarian, making the leap to being on a fully plant-based diet involves giving up dairy and eggs. In the investigations I have done so far, I don't see any compelling evidence to entirely cut these out of my diet from a health or biological point of view. I could certainly do with reducing my consumption of animal products, though. Even the environmental or economic arguments show that compared to taking meat off the table, moving from vegetarian to vegan has a small impact.

The real issue seems that the milk and egg industries mistreat the animals to meet the levels of demand and turn a profit. Returning to the thought experiment from earlier, I'm still content to take a bit of milk from a happy, healthy cow. However, am I willing to artificially inseminate the cow so she has a calf to keep her lactating? Maybe, though perhaps by introducing her to a nice bull at the right time of year. Am I willing to then strip her calf away from her so I can have lots of milk? No, this seems greedy. Then am I willing to kill her calf, and her as well after a few years when I no longer need her milk? No, this would be cruel.

Curiously, the real question here seems to be *what amount* of dairy and eggs to consume. Clearly, a vegan would say "none". From a health point of view, it seems OK to consume a bit. From a moral and economic point of view, however, I am curious about what amounts of milk and eggs can be obtained by keeping animals ourselves and looking after them in a cruelty-free way.

So, we want to compute roughly how much milk we can get while being as kind as possible to the cows. For eggs, there already seems to be a trend to keep chickens in the back garden if one has the space. Perhaps we can calculate how many eggs we can get if we have a contently clucking flock of chickens.

A "cowputation"

Is it possible to keep a herd of cattle in a way that doesn't require slaughtering them and allows the calves to drink milk naturally? I'm going to make certain assumptions here, round the numbers, and ignore the practicalities of looking after bulls and cows together. It's just to get an idea of how much milk we could expect to receive by keeping a cow. Would we be bathing in it, or just have enough to splash on our cereal in the morning?

The average cow lives for about twenty years. We would not send her to slaughter, so we would need to look after her for twenty years. Cows lactate for about ten months but need to give birth to a calf to lactate[16]. So, if we want a constant supply of milk, a new calf needs to be born every ten months. As we never slaughter an animal, we would have about twenty-four cows all ten months apart in age. About half the animals would be bulls, so obviously they wouldn't produce milk,

---

[16] Oddly, until about fifteen years ago, I hadn't really thought about this and assumed that cows just always "gave" milk. This is why in my teenaged thought experiment I didn't specify that the cow had to be lactating.

but we would keep them as part of the herd. On average, each cow would only need to give birth to two calves in its life, meaning the specific cow producing milk would not need to be pregnant again for a while. This may mean a difference in the levels of hormones in the milk, as in most modern systems cows are pregnant with their next calf whilst still being milked. Let's round our numbers and say we maintain a herd of twenty-five animals.

Now we need to figure out how much milk a cow can produce. An article in Farmers Weekly about a farm that managed to massively increase its yields[1] stated that before "improving their infrastructure and technology", it would average 7,500 litres per cow per year. They managed to nearly double this by using milking robots, keeping the cows indoors all year round, and strictly controlling their diets. Cows lactate for about ten months, which is about 300 days. So the farm in question was getting about twenty-five litres of milk from each cow on a daily basis over a ten-month period. I want to cross-check this number. Arla Foods, a Danish multinational cooperative, is known for high animal welfare levels. Arla say their cows are not given hormones to increase yields and are treated well. Their cows average twenty to thirty litres of milk a day[2]. Another source says the average is around twenty-eight litres a day over ten months[3]. So about twenty-five litres a day, and therefore 7,500 litres a year, seems to make sense.

From that 7,500 litres, we should let the calf drink its share. If we are not artificially weaning, then it seems calves naturally wean in about ten months[4],[5]. That makes sense—it is roughly how long their mother's lactate! Calves drink about 20% of their body weight in milk to begin with, and drop to about 14% by one month of age[6]. After this, the amount of milk consumed drops quite rapidly[7]. Let's assume from month two to ten, the milk required as a percentage of body weight drops from 9% to 1%—i.e., a two-month-old calf drinks 9% of its body weight, a three-month-old drinks 8%, and by the time it is ten months old, it drinks 1%. This probably over-estimates how much milk the calf drinks, but we want there to be plenty available for it.

At the same time, the calf will be growing. Calves are about 40kg when born and weigh about 270kg by ten months. Assuming linear growth (it isn't really, but this is "back of an envelope mathematics"), that means on day one, a 40kg calf drinking 20% should consume about 8kg per day. By one month, their weight is about 60kg, they should drink about 14%, so about 8.4kg of milk. Going linearly from here (increasing weight linearly, and dropping the percentage of bodyweight drunk), we end up with about 2,400kg of milk drunk by the calf over ten months. The density of milk is about $1.03kg/cm^3$, which gets us to about 2,300 litres. This is probably already an overestimate, but to keep the numbers simple, let's round up to 2,500 litres. We want to make sure the calf is allowed to drink as much milk as it likes.

The "excess milk" left over for us is about 5,000 litres. That's spread over about 300 days, so we get between sixteen and seventeen litres of extra milk a day whilst the cow is lactating.

So, if you maintain a herd of twenty-five cattle, making sure that at any point in time one cow is lactating, and let all the animals live out their lives, you would expect to get about 16-17 litres of milk a day. That's quite a lot. Also, every ten months or so, a cow would die of old age, so some meat and leather could be harvested "guilt-free".

Looking after twenty-five cows and bulls would be quite an undertaking, so what about the traditional Hindu idea of keeping a cow as a "family member"? Consider a village of twenty-five families. Each household looks after one animal, and between them, they ensure one cow is always lactating. Whichever family has the oldest cow gets the newest calf after weaning. As part of this arrangement, each household would get about 650ml (or just over one pint) of milk a day. That's just about three glasses a day for the whole family. It's not a whole lot. Also, in this scenario, each family would get one dead animal (so meat and leather) once every twenty years. Although, if they have a relationship with the cow, they may opt not to harvest these products.

Now let us consider a herd of twenty-five cattle with modern intensive farming techniques. The farm in the Farmers Weekly article increased production to 14,500 litres a year per cow. These yield figures are ever increasing; other sources claim certain breeds can produce up to 17,000 litres[8] or even over 30,000 litres[9] over a year. We'll assume we manage an even 20,000 litres per cow per year. Let's say we have twenty-five cows (we can get bull semen for artificial insemination without having to look after the bull year-round). All twenty-five cows would be impregnated, give birth, and lactate on an annual basis. So, in one year, twenty-five cows would each produce 20,000 litres of milk giving a total of 500,000 litres. Split over a calendar year, this is 1,370 litres per day. That means using the same herd size (and therefore for a similar underlying cost), a mass-production type system would produce about ninety times more milk than a completely compassionate method. This means that the cost of totally ethical milk should be about nearly ninety times more than what we can buy in the shops. This method also produces twenty-five calves each year, many of which can be sold. The fully grown cows would also be slaughtered every few years, so a lot of meat and leather could be produced and sold. This would probably subsidise the cost of the intensively farmed milk further. Obviously, these are very rough figures, but the order of magnitude is probably correct. So, we can say for sure that you can get "tens of times more milk" with intensive farming. Perhaps my number is right, and it's ninety times, perhaps it's something like fifty, or something as high as 150. Either way, it's probably not as low as three or four.

That felt like an interview question! Here's is a summary.

Table 1: Comparing milk yields under different methods of care

		No Harm Farming	Non-Intensive Farming	Intensive Farming
	Period to consider[17]	300 days	1 year	1 year
Milk (L) over whole period	Yield per cow	7,500	7,500	20,000
	Given to calf	2,500	n/a	n/a
	Excess for humans	5,000	7,500	20,000
	Yield from herd of 25	5,000	187,500	500,000
	Milk (L) per day	17	514	1,370
	Relative production	1.2%	37.5%	"100%"

---

17 In our compassionate care method, we only have one lactating cow in the herd. When she stops producing milk, we immediately start the next cow so the supply is "continuous". For other methods, each member of the herd lactates for ten months then is dried off for two months before giving birth and starting to lactate again. The supply can be made continuous by staggering the pregnancies of each cow, but the ten-month supply from each cow is spread out over a whole calendar year.

Clearly, when being as kind as possible to the animals, the availability of milk is limited. Perhaps this is why traditionally milk was so highly valued in India. Being so hard to come by, one can understand that a family's ritual offering of milk would be seen as making a greater sacrifice. For a lot of families in rural India who keep cows, this is probably still true. However, most people reading this do not keep a cow in the garden, do not lovingly care for it, nurture it, look after its calf, and humbly ask for a bit of extra milk after the calf has drunk its fill. We pop into the supermarket and pick up a four-pint bottle of blue top. Using ever-increasing amounts of milk in rituals reminds me of the parable of the Widow's Offering from the Bible (Mark 12:41-44). In the story, a poor widow donates two small copper coins to the temple. The wealthy who could give bags of gold were said to be showing less devotion as they donated from their surplus, whilst she had given nearly all she had.

So we need to ask ourselves: when it comes to performing rituals, is there more value in the milk obtained by lovingly looking after a cow yourself, or the supermarket milk which was probably obtained in a way that exploits and harms the cows that helped to produce it? From a pragmatic point of view, one could argue that using the supermarket milk in rituals is akin to the able-bodied person using a *paakli* to reach the Vaishno Devi temple. In other words, it is dogmatically sticking to a cultural tradition but doing it in a way that is the most convenient by shortcutting the traditional "payment". It is no longer giving up milk that is obtained by lovingly looking after a "mother cow", but instead by treating the cow as a milk factory.

A "cluckulation"

Whilst milk could be obtained in a very humane way, the key issue is that to obtain milk, a new calf must be brought into existence. If we increase milk consumption to a rate where there are too many calves, then we need to do something with them. The current commercial solution is to slaughter them or deny them their mother's milk. Eggs are a bit different.

Hens naturally produce eggs on a regular basis. They also moult in the autumn as the days get shorter. The process takes about ten weeks as they shed their feathers and grow new ones. During this time, they stop laying eggs as their reproductive systems also "reset". To maintain supply, farmers can either use artificial lighting to trick the hens into thinking autumn hasn't kicked in yet (so they moult later in the year), or they can force moulting earlier by putting the hen through some stress (like starving her for a while).

On most commercial egg farms, hens produce an egg every day or two whilst they are not moulting. Even if the eggs are unfertilised and therefore not a living creature, they are full of enough nutrition to sustain and grow a chick over about three weeks with no other food source. There is an issue with this rate of production: if a hen produces a self-contained egg which could create a chick nearly every day, she needs to consume nutrition in proportion with this. We know from our earlier research that to produce an egg, the hen needs to consume nearly four times as much protein and calories.

Eggshells are made up essentially of calcium carbonate. This is used in bones, and there has actually been work to try to use eggshells to help mend bone fractures in humans[10]. Without proper nutrition, the burden of creating an eggshell every day or two can lead to calcium deficiency, leaving chickens with weak bones.

In fact, when left alone, chickens will consume their own unfertilised eggs to replenish their nutrients. Before baulking at this idea, it's worth noting that in nature many mammals eat their placentae[11]. In fact, some (admittedly very few) women opt to consume their placenta after childbirth[12]. It's been helping to keep their baby alive for the last nine months and is full of residual nutrients.

So how come hens produce eggs at such an alarming and potentially harmful rate? Well, that's our fault. Over generations, we have selectively bred chickens that have faster reproductive cycles. Wild relatives of chickens generally produce about one egg a month[13]. That is a vast difference.

Let's try to calculate how many eggs we could expect to receive if looking after chickens ourselves. This should be a little simpler as there is no dependence on creating a living being to produce eggs; we'd just need chicks to replace the older chickens.

Hens can lay eggs for most of their lives, but after the first year or two, the rate at which they produce eggs begins to drop. This is why, in the egg industry, most hens are slaughtered at this point. Egg production continues to decline with age, and there is some data about the kind of drop in production one can expect[14]. Chickens can live for quite some time, as long as ten years — with one famous hen reaching sixteen years[15]. In other words, we will be looking after them for quite some time.

Let's say we go with a backyard chicken breed that produces about 200 eggs in its first year of laying. With a ten-week moulting period thrown in, those 200 eggs are spread over about 300 days, so it's roughly two eggs every three days whilst she's laying.

Chickens are social animals, so it's best to keep more than one. If we want to always have one that is producing eggs at an optimal rate, we should get a new hen every two years. If they live for ten years, this means we will have five hens each two years apart. So our egg production would vary on a two-year cycle and look something like this:

Table 2: Egg production across hens of different ages

Year	Age of chickens (years)				Eggs per		
	1-2	3-4	5-6	7-8	300 days	day	
1	200	126	100	72	498	1.7	5 eggs every 3 days
2	166	118	86	62	432	1.4	About 3 eggs every 2 days

We are ignoring the oldest hen; she would be over eight-years-old and may well have died or, according to some sources, have stopped producing eggs. If she's still alive and laying, then we will consider her eggs a bonus, but they don't change the numbers much.

There are a couple of additional considerations. Every two years, we can't guarantee that the new chicken will be female. So to keep things simple, let's say we get two new chickens, and on average we get one male and one female (not guaranteed but hopefully true on average). Because we are not slaughtering the male chicks, our flock will actually consist of ten birds: five male-female pairs each two years apart. Now things are getting tricky. Too many cockerels and not enough hens in a small back garden can cause issues, especially as each of the cockerels tries to assert his dominance. This would have been an issue with bulls as well, but we ignored it then, so we will ignore it now.

The other aspect to manage is "birth control". Once a cockerel and hen mate, the hen may produce fertilised eggs for up to two weeks. A young hen may produce ten eggs over this time! If we want to get only two new chicks, then we need a hen that only produces about two or three eggs over a fortnight. This would have to be amongst our oldest hens (the seven- or eight-year-olds). As they would only produce about one egg every four to five days, so only two or three fertilised eggs over a fortnight. The alternative is to take all eggs laid by the hen over this period and only incubate two of them. But as the eggs are fertilised and you are not allowing them to grow, you may get into discussions about whether this amounts to abortion.

By keeping ten chickens, we could expect on average to get about 450 eggs over one year. That's forty-five eggs per year per chicken. Considering the ten-week moulting period, this means about one egg a week outside of autumn. We would also get an old dead chicken about once a year that could be used for meat.

Now let's consider a flock of ten hens in a commercial setting. Commercial breeds can produce upward of 280 eggs a year when young, so you would get about 2,800 eggs a year. This high-volume production would involve getting rid of chickens after a year or two and discarding almost all male chicks. So completely slaughter-free eggs would probably cost about six times more than commercial ones.

If we compare this with our milk calculation we find the level of "harm" in commercial milk farming is much higher than the level of harm in commercial egg farming. This is interesting as there are some vegetarians who will not eat eggs but happily drink milk

Decision time

Having strung you along on my meandering journey towards veganism for the last ninety pages it is time to make a final decision. Let's revisit some of the main points that we have covered. As I mentioned, my personal ethic is grounded in Hindu philosophy, but it's always good to go back to some of your well-established beliefs and habits to re-assess them. I see this as a core part of why the Hindu tradition has survived for so long; it has some core principles but adapts its practices to match the times. I mentioned trying to be more aware of the consequences of one's actions. For me, this idea stems from Karma, but rather than dwelling on intangible consequences, I try to think more deeply about how my actions affect the real world. This means being compassionate, not only by respecting the life and liberty of other living beings, but also by respecting decisions made by other people that may differ from mine.

At its core, the vegan view is that all living beings should be protected from unnecessary harm or exploitation. In practice some vegans will look for a "list of instructions" on how to behave as a vegan[18], others will try to follow vegan principles when making decisions. I find I have always agreed with the ethos of veganism, but I wonder if the practice can be taken a bit too far. The practical push of some vegans seems to be that humans should live completely separately from the rest of the animal kingdom, even though we are "just animals" ourselves. Some vegans object to keeping pets. Those who do choose to live with a companion animal often rescue one from a shelter rather than buying one from a breeder or pet shop. The logic being that animals in shelters are abandoned and being left to suffer, so a vegan can alleviate the animal's suffering by looking after it. Whereas buying a pet involves thinking of the animal as property, and often means an animal was brought into existence just so that it can live

---

[18] Try letting your favourite search engine complete the phrase "Can vegans eat…" or "Can vegans use…"to get an idea of what other people have asked.

as a pet. Essentially, they object to the animals being unnecessarily commoditised.

Whilst the Hindu principle is similar (e.g., that we are all living beings deserving of respect and protection from harm), there is a difference in the end practice. The Hindu view involves the idea that we cannot separate ourselves from the natural world. We are all connected. As such, the cow is a living being, we are also living beings, and we can live in a symbiotic relationship with animals. So as a member of the family, the cow is treated well. Lord Krishna famously would take cows to pasture, play his flute for them, and look after them. He also fondly consumed butter churned from their milk. The cow produces milk for its calf, and the calf is allowed to drink; we only take the extra milk.

First-time human mothers often worry about not producing enough milk for their offspring, and they are told about the supply-and-demand of milk production. If a mother has twins, her body produces more milk as the babies demand more. In the same way, the cow feeds her calf first, then we (as her other children) come asking for some extra milk, which she will be able to provide. This would explain why the cow-mother analogy is so strong in Hinduism. We should be thankful for this gift and not take too much.

Over time Hindu practices have changed, with certain rituals being removed, modified or added. Animal sacrifice has more or less stopped. Traditionally lamps were lit for Diwali, yet now some people feel the only way to celebrate is with loud, extravagant fireworks. There is no mention of the practice of Satipratha (widow sacrifice) in the Vedas, and yet it became so ingrained as a societal ritual that laws had to be written to ban it. So perhaps when a ritual asks for milk, yoghurt, or honey, we can use a non-animal derived alternative. When we feel like making a traditional milk-based dish, we can use something plant-based instead.

Let's briefly return to thinking about the consequences of our actions. Using milk and eggs doesn't intrinsically harm animals, so I would argue that the use of these is not morally wrong. The moral issues come from how these products are obtained. It seems like the mass production of milk and eggs to meet consumer demand has meant the processes used to procure them are causing harm to living beings. We could argue that if enough consumers demanded a change in practices, then the industries would have to follow suit. This may be true, but we still have an issue with the level of production required. As we found in our rough calculations, to produce the same amount of milk in a completely harm-free way would probably require ninety times as many cows and bulls. To produce the same numbers of eggs, may need six times as many chickens. When we consider that we would not want to cage these animals, we realise the sheer space required to keep them all would be impractical.

So the only real option to help protect the animals from harm is a massive reduction in the consumption of animal products. Keeping track of this at a personal level can be difficult, but there are various regulated ways to make a change. Vegans choose to reduce their consumption to zero. Some people may set certain times to eat fully plant-based food, either by doing Veganuary, where they are vegan for a single month, or avoiding certain products on specific days of the week. This is fine so long as people don't compensate by eating extra animal products on their off days. Others choose to go "Chegan", eating fully plant-based most of the time, but allowing themselves a cheat day or a cheat food. This may work better depending on how people do it. Having one cheat day in a month would hopefully not mean eating thirty days' worth of animal products in one go!

So am I now fully vegan?

Not quite – but whilst writing this book I have been making changes! Being vegetarian already, at this stage I have not become a strict vegan who completely cuts out dairy and eggs. I'm now aware of the kind of exploitation that goes into producing milk and eggs at our current levels of consumption. So I have been trying to reduce my consumption of them to a more sustainable level. If there is a vegan option, I aim to make it my preference. I have shifted to non-dairy milk at home and make it my choice when it's available elsewhere. Given the numbers that came out in our calculations, I am making a reduction in my consumption of eggs, but essentially trying to think of them as an expensive ingredient, rather than a staple food.

The next time someone asks about my dietary choices, hopefully I can avoid the blind panic I used to feel as a teenager. I may still use my "*You are walking home late one evening*" scenario. Perhaps we can discuss the environmental or economic impact of what we choose to eat. Maybe they are the kind of person up for a discussion on morality. In any case, we would have an opportunity for some really interesting mealtime conversation!

References

You are what you eat or what you don't

[1] Lisa the Vegetarian. The Simpsons (Season 7, Episode 5) (First aired 15th October 1995). Gracie Films; Twentieth Century Fox Film Corporation.

[2] Wiseman, J., 2014. SAS Survival Handbook: The Ultimate Guide to Surviving Anywhere. HarperCollins

Feasting, fasting and philosophy

[1] The Vegan Society. 2020. Definition Of Veganism. [online] Available at: <https://www.vegansociety.com/go-vegan/definition-veganism> [Accessed 31 August 2020].

[2] Censusindia.gov.in. 2020. Census Of India Website : Office Of The Registrar General & Census Commissioner, India. [online] Available at: <https://censusindia.gov.in/2011census/Religion_PCA.html> [Accessed 31 August 2020].

[3] Shridhar, K., Dhillon, P., Bowen, L., Kinra, S., Bharathi, A., Prabhakaran, D., Reddy, K. and Ebrahim, S., 2014. Nutritional profile of Indian vegetarian diets – the Indian Migration Study (IMS). Nutrition Journal, 13(1)

[4] En.wikipedia.org. 2020. Vegetarianism By Country. [online] Available at: <https://en.wikipedia.org/wiki/Vegetarianism_by_country> [Accessed 31 August 2020].

[5] Radhakrishnan, S., 2014. The Principal Upaniṣads: HarperCollins Publishers.

Choices, choices

[1] Business Insider. 2020. These 19 Elite Athletes Are Vegan — Here's What Made Them Switch Their Diet. [online] Available at: <https://www.businessinsider.com/vegan-athletes-and-why-they-changed-their-diet-11> [Accessed 31 August 2020].

[2] The Game Changers. 2018. Film.

[3] Mach, W., Thimmesch, A., Pierce, J. and Pierce, J., 2011. Consequences of Hyperoxia and the Toxicity of Oxygen in the Lung. Nursing Research and Practice, 2011, pp.1-7.

[4] The One With the Breast Milk. Friends (Series 2, Episode 2) (First aired 28th September 1995). Warner Bros. Television Distribution.

[5] Oppenlander, R., 2012. Comfortably Unaware. Beaufort Books.

[6] Robbins, J., 2012. Diet For A New America. H J Kramer, pp.326-327.

[7] Steinfeld, H., 2006. Livestock's Long Shadow. Rome: Food and Agriculture Organization of the United Nations, p.xxi.

[8] US EPA. 2020. Global Greenhouse Gas Emissions Data | US EPA. [online] Available at: <https://www.epa.gov/ghgemissions/global-greenhouse-gas-emissions-data#Sector> [Accessed 31 August 2020].

[9] Jones, N., Conklin, A., Suhrcke, M. and Monsivais, P., 2014. The Growing Price Gap between More and Less Healthy Foods: Analysis of a Novel Longitudinal UK Dataset. PLoS ONE, 9(10), p.e109343.

[10] Theproteinworks.com. 2020. What Are The Best Cheap Sources Of Protein? Get The Most Bang For Your Buck With Our Top 15. | The Protein Works. [online] Available at: <https://www.theproteinworks.com/thelockerroom/what-are-the-best-cheap-sources-of-protein-get-the-most-bang-for-your-buck-with-our-top-15/> [Accessed 31 August 2020].

[11] Coach.nine.com.au. 2020. 20 Of The Cheapest Protein Sources, Ranked By Cost. [online] Available at: <https://coach.nine.com.au/diet/the-cheapest-sources-of-protein/5e754184-24fe-4254-b437-19a6f5a59bbf> [Accessed 31 August 2020].

[12] Our World in Data. 2020. Protein Efficiency Of Meat And Dairy Production. [online] Available at: <https://ourworldindata.org/grapher/protein-efficiency-of-meat-and-dairy-production> [Accessed 31 August 2020].

[13] Our World in Data. 2020. Energy Efficiency Of Meat And Dairy Production. [online] Available at: <https://ourworldindata.org/grapher/energy-efficiency-of-meat-and-dairy-production> [Accessed 31 August 2020].

[14] Full Fact. 2020. Do Farmers Make More From Subsidies Than Agriculture?. [online] Available at: <https://fullfact.org/economy/farming-subsidies-uk/> [Accessed 31 August 2020].

[15] Agrismart. 2020. Farming Subsidies - Are They Worth More To Farmers Than Agricultural Revenue? - Agrismart. [online] Available at: <https://www.agrismart.co.uk/farming-subsidies-are-they-worth-more-to-farmers-than-agricultural-revenue/> [Accessed 31 August 2020].

[16] Our World in Data. 2020. Milk Production. [online] Available at: <https://ourworldindata.org/grapher/milk-production?tab=chart&country=~IND> [Accessed 31 August 2020].

[17] National Dairy Development Board, 2020. Operation Flood | Nddb.Coop. [online] Available at: <https://www.nddb.coop/about/genesis/flood> [Accessed 31 August 2020].

[18] Smith, J., 2020. Vegan Celebrities Who Are Inspiring Us To Adopt A Plant-Based Diet During Isolation. [online] Glamour UK. Available at: <https://www.glamourmagazine.co.uk/gallery/celebrities-who-are-vegan> [Accessed 31 August 2020].

[19] Hidden Figures. 2016. 20th Century Fox. Film.

Veganism - Beyond diet

[1] En.wikipedia.org. 2020. Ahimsa Silk. [online] Available at: <https://en.wikipedia.org/wiki/Ahimsa_silk> [Accessed 31 August 2020].

[2] Ahimsamilk.org. 2020. Ahimsa Milk – Slaughter Free Milk. [online] Available at: <https://www.ahimsamilk.org/> [Accessed 31 August 2020].

[3] Joy, M., 2011. Why We Love Dogs, Eat Pigs And Wear Cows. Conari Press.

Veggie to Vegan: A leap of faith?

[1] Price, R., 2020. How UK Herd Achieved World Top 10 Ranking For Milk Yield - Farmers Weekly. [online] Farmers Weekly. Available at: <https://www.fwi.co.uk/livestock/uk-herd-achieved-world-top-10-ranking-for-milk-yield> [Accessed 31 August 2020].

[2] 2020. Our Farms - Happy Cows Are Healthy Cows. [online] Available at: <https://www.arlafoods.co.uk/about-arla/our-farms/#happy-cows-are-healthy-cows> [Accessed 31 August 2020].

[3] 2020. Standard Intenstive Milk Production. [online] Available at: <https://www.compassioninfoodbusiness.com/awards/good-dairy-award/standard-intenstive-milk-production/> [Accessed 31 August 2020].

[4] Lewis, D., 2020. New Way To Wean Calves Leaves Them Happier And Healthier. [online] Smithsonian Magazine. Available at: <https://www.smithsonianmag.com/smart-news/new-way-wean-calves-leaves-them-happier-healthier-180957919> [Accessed 31 August 2020].

[5] Animals.mom.me. 2020. What Happens If You Don't Wean Calves?. [online] Available at: <https://animals.mom.me/happens-dont-wean-calves-9821.html> [Accessed 31 August 2020].

[6] Milkproduction.com. 2020. How Much Milk Will Calves Drink? - Milkproduction.Com. [online] Available at: <http://www.milkproduction.com/Library/Scientific-articles/Calf-Management/How-much-milk-will-calves-drink/> [Accessed 31 August 2020].

[7] Jasper, J. and Weary, D., 2002. Effects of Ad Libitum Milk Intake on Dairy Calves. Journal of Dairy Science, 85(11), pp.3054-3058.

[8] En.wikipedia.org. 2020. Dairy Cattle. [online] Available at: <https://en.wikipedia.org/wiki/Dairy_cattle#Milk_production_levels> [Accessed 31 August 2020]

[9] Rai, A., 2020. Top 10 Highest Milk Producing Cattle Breeds In All Over The World. [online] ABLTechnology. Available at: <https://abltechnology.wordpress.com/2015/06/12/top-10-highest-milk-producing-cattle-breeds-in-all-over-the-world/> [Accessed 31 August 2020].

[10] Wu, X., Stroll, S., Lantigua, D., Suvarnapathaki, S. and Camci-Unal, G., 2019. Eggshell particle-reinforced hydrogels for bone tissue engineering: an orthogonal approach. Biomaterials Science, 7(7), pp.2675-2685.

[11] Kristal, M., 1980. Placentophagia: A biobehavioral enigma (or De gustibus non disputandum est). Neuroscience & Biobehavioral Reviews, 4(2), pp.141-150.

[12] Hayes, E., 2016. Consumption of the Placenta in the Postpartum Period. Journal of Obstetric, Gynecologic & Neonatal Nursing, 45(1), pp.78-89.

[13] Romanov, M. and Weigend, S., 2001. Analysis of Genetic Relationships Between Various Populations of Domestic and Jungle Fowl Using Microsatellite Markers. Poultry Science, 80(8), pp.1057-1063.

[14] 2019. 10 Breeds Of Chicken That Will Lay Lots Of Eggs For You. [online] Thehappychickencoop.com. Available at: <https://www.thehappychickencoop.com/10-breeds-of-chicken-that-will-lay-lots-of-eggs-for-you> [Accessed 31 August 2020].

[15] En.wikipedia.org. 2020. Matilda (Chicken). [online] Available at: <https://en.wikipedia.org/wiki/Matilda_(chicken)> [Accessed 31 August 2020].

Acknowledgements

This book is the result of months of work (and only part of it by me!). In particular, I must thank Vibhuti Patel, my mentor during this writing journey, and especially in helping me to turn a "stream of consciousness" into something more structured that I hope you will have enjoyed reading.

Secondly, I have to thank my wife, Anjali. This book was very much written during the height of the Covid-19 lockdown in the UK. Both Anjali and I were working from home, and home-schooling our daughters. After all of that she would permit me some time in the evenings and the weekends to get this written – whilst also revising for medical exams herself. Exams which she has gone on to pass!

TATTVA
PRESS